Real Indian
Junk Jewelry

Real Indian
Junk Jewelry

Trevino L. Brings Plenty

The Backwaters Press

First Printing: February 2012

Published by: The Backwaters Press
                       Greg Kosmicki, Rich Wyatt, Editors
                       3502 N. 52nd Street
                       Omaha, Nebraska 68104-3506

                       thebackwaterspress@gmail.com
                       http://www.thebackwaterspress.org

                       ISBN: 978-1-935218-28-9

Acknowledgments

Some of the poems in this book have appeared in *Open Wide Magazine* #12 and the *Portland Alliance*.

Thanks much to:
My family and friends for their support. I would especially like to thank my wife for the long-term care of my psyche and the intimate nature of our emotional struggles. How we complement each other will pull us through this life.

Contents

1

For the Sake of Beauty   3

Don't Believe in Your Dreams   4

Stoic Pity   5

She Made the First Move   6

Baking the Future   7

Scalping the Sorrow   8

The Sound of It   9

Taking Advantage   10

The I Poem   11

A Woman as Cold as Ice   12

Accounts of Love   13

Antiques   15

After a Fuck   16

To Know and Understand   17

Indian Woman   18

The Fingers   19

Tracing the Source   20

An American Indian Love in a Western Novel   21

I Was Your Crazy Horse   22

Motel Bed   23

To Play It Cool   24

Broken Treaties   25

The Visit   26

Matilda in Portland, Oregon   27

One Bad Night   29

Mona Lisa's Smile   30

Love   32

Poems Not as Good as Money   33

Love and Hate Are in the Same Hand   34

Friends, Lovers   35

2

My Pony   39
Indian Spirit Guide   40
Excerpt from the Diary of Sitting Bull   41
The Last Great Indian Casanova   42
Zombie Love   43
Add It Up   44
Matchstick Tribe   45
Boredom   46
Slam Poetry   47
Birthday Party Sweater   48
Secondhand Underwear   49
John Wayne Instinct   50
Real Indian Junk Jewelry   51
What's Your Background?   52

3

Let Them Rage   57
Again the Air was Thin   58
Before Turning 27   59
Portland Lights   60
This is Where I Grew and Lived   61
Street Ghosts   62
Lorca and I   63
My Lover, Death   64
The Rusted, Red Wheelbarrow   65
The Writing Process   66
Meditation   67
Truths   68
Who Else Has Been Here   69
Neruda   70
Old Man 27   71
Wedding Music   72
When It Finally Comes   73
What They Wanted   74

4

The Old Moan   77

Fear's Endurance   78

Intertribal Street   80

Blood on the Basket   82

The Ways of Medicine   84

George Finds Medicine   86

Deer Soup, Fry Bread, *Wojape*   87

Manifest Bus Destination   88

Four Ways of Looking at a Red Cowboy   89

Becoming a Good End   91

Work Is Finished   93

Dancers   94

Bus Stop   96

I Am in the Reservation of My Mind   98

9/64   101

Lakotas Die in the Northwest   102

The Sleeping   104

Wounded Knee Opus   106

Stationary Rescue   108

Acts of Kindness   109

December Seventh, Two Thousand and One   110

About the Poet   113

For those destroyed by and in America.

1

She is red onion paper
in a pond
sinking to a dark bottom
and then
she is gone
in the ripples' calm disappearance.

For the Sake of Beauty

On the phone I asked her to wear a full buckskin outfit and she could be the beauty that would make me steal horses.

She said she didn't have a buckskin outfit.

I said I would make her one, but use pages from books.

A week later when she came over to my place, she asked if I had made an outfit.

I said no. I couldn't bring myself to hunt the books on my shelf, even if it were for food or clothing. I couldn't bring myself to kill, even for the sake of beauty.

Don't Believe in Your Dreams

Later, you said in a dream you looked for me under a star quilt. I wasn't there and when you woke I still wasn't there.

In my dream, I played trumpet with Coltrane on the balcony of a cheap New York tenement.

You called me that night. I let the answering machine pick you up.

Stoic Pity

My big Indian heart was fractured, stomach pangs screamed, but I'm Indian and this should be a natural act: a dead Indian man in love with a you who can't live in me.

When I threw up this time there was blood. I've learned to destroy this body. All my relations showed their way of making flesh vanish like rose petals down a stream.

I forgot some days to sleep and walked away from solitude when I had cheap beer and whiskey and lived on daily rations of potatoes and rice.

As I looked at my chunky bile with an iron taste in my mouth, and the stench of beer on my breath, I believed the words that made your mistakes. You said I was handsome. I didn't believe you because when you lied you were beautiful.

You weren't there, but I wanted you at my side because one thing Indians do well is mourn.

I can't stop drinking of the closest friend kept next to the bed on top of my book of longing. I don't want to end the wilted leaf that is addiction.

Some mornings I wanted to sing the blues, but my voice was rusted and some nights I didn't want to sleep, but those were nights I passed out.

I needed to talk with you, the one who destroyed this city and contaminated the soil of me.

You who I walked away from without another word and made long conversations with beer cans and dope in the creases of night.

It has always been you who I am afraid to hear are doing well.

She Made the First Move

I'm a simple man, my love. A man of drink and laugh and any
complication is only kindling.

She, a woman with a soft face and subtle mannerisms has a passion for
life like a rain forest on fire.

This graceful, mad love, let me out of your chains. I have reason to
travel with self only. This song she sings—I don't want to know
its contour.

I release you, she says. I release you.

She releases me and I split in half.

Retie me, I cry. Retie me.

Baking the Future

She wrapped foil around two salmon steaks, put them in the pre-heated oven and we waited.

I opened another bottle of red wine, threw the empty one in the kitchen sink filled with dirty dishes.

She laid two paper plates on a small table that was scratched from a previous life in a local pizza pub.

The Indians of the Columbia River viciously ate salmon and I hoped that both of us, as we sat across from each other, would have genetic memory and eat the flesh without any intimidation.

I wanted to say a prayer for the salmon she placed on the paper plates, but instead I made a toast to big, bad love.

Scalping the Sorrow

My woman don't treat me no good. She only brought trouble and heartache and in a drug and alcohol induced rage I cut my hair with a knife 'cause I ain't longer be her one and only man.

The Sound of It

When you spoke of it you sounded the explosion, the skyline, love's water rush, the wilted fist, the scream of a desert, the cracked moon, and oblivion's color. You spoke of the dark, blue night around my eyes.

Taking Advantage

She lies next to me in bed. I touch her skin. I think she dreams I might give up. No, I am physically here, not a forever, but long enough.

The lights are off, the shades are open. I look out the window and see the waxing moon cut through the sky. I am looking home. I am to be another light for someone else to look toward.

She lies next to me dreaming I'll cease and fully turn to her. No, I have my work to do, I have to till these pages, knead these books.

I have been looking up too often. My works are collecting dust. Poetry needs more than a lover, poetry needs a friend.

The I Poem

There you stood among trees. I thought you a poem, but that was too sentimental. Damn, trees surrounded by cement sidewalks, traffic stinking the air, the damn city intervened, it was all not welcomed.

I saw you standing there, child at your side. I wanted to touch your face and pat his head, say hello, but who was I to intrude in your life, again.

I was ground rock slopped together, a metal machine alive on fumes. I was only passing. That was all. I was not permanent, nor welcomed. But you didn't want to hear this. You wanted a damn poem. Damn, I wanted a poem. I wanted something in this world permanent and reliable. I wanted to stand on a corner in the South Park blocks of downtown Portland and have someone see me and write it down.

But that wouldn't be nice. It wouldn't even be sincere. It was always best to stand while life drove on by than to stop a moment to stop all the moments.

A Woman as Cold as Ice

You see, she wanted me dead. Her arms were like snares and legs like nets. She was cute and nice, but that wasn't good enough. She was still dumb with a nasally voice and had about her a putrid, musky flower scent. I knew when I met her she was trouble, but I fell right in anyways.

She wanted me dead, I could tell. I heard it in her voice. Sure, she said, "I love you," but really I heard, "I would love you dead." She was cute and nice I give her that, but that doesn't cut it.

Now, she is a spider and I am a fly stuck in her fucked-up web. She is waiting for me, damn her, to tire, then she will wrap me up and suck out the rest of my life.

Accounts of Love

1.
I loved the way you smoked a cigarette after sex then drilled it into
my chest.

2.
After a long night of drinking, the heartburn I had was just like your
love: uninvited and predictable.

3.
I loved the way your pelvic bone grabbed my cock like a noose and the
Jaws of Life.

4.
I loved you like a beer bottle busted on a countertop and thrust in
my face.

5.
It was a drunken drive home on muscle relaxants. This was your love,
it was not giving a shit and with nothing but big hopes.

6.
I went down to Famine Street, there I had love in my hands, it was a
beautiful dead bird that would never fly again.

7.
I was headed to New York to see the Atlantic Ocean, throw this love
from the Brooklyn Bridge, but you know this could be anywhere.

8.
My car broke down and I walked home drunk, 10 miles. The blisters on
my feet were like your love, limited and hurt ever yard.

9.
I gave up on water, sipped cheap wine, slit my wrist, and wanted to die with the sunrise.

10.
At 3:10 a.m., I tapped on your window, but you took the 3 a.m. train to Chicago. This was my love, nobody home and too late.

11.
The need was like a bullet in the head. I sold my soul. O Lord, I would fall to the sky if this was love and not the report of a Saturday Special.

12.
I was here in love with nightmares, horse bones, and the desires of wishes.

13.
This last summer, this last love, I'll give another chance when this body is blue. Put me in an unmarked hole beneath a low, bent oak tree.

14.
People might laugh, but there was nothing funny about a drunk who loved loss.

Antiques

I want to live in truth, blow the settled dust, strip the flesh, and show only bone. It is the granules of who we are. There are too many facts. Let them glow in silence's comfort.

I look you over real good. Yeah, I would like to fall apart with you. We would smile with sagged skin, hair gray and balding, and dentures in our mouths.

In memory we live our youth and with you, I want to let those years loosen with the coming old age. Yes, together drift into eternity.

After a Fuck

"I don't trust you," I said.

"Why?" she asked.

"You are the one I love," I answered. "That's a lot to ask from me."

"You're so sweet. That is why I love an Indian poet. You have nothing but yourself to give."

"No, I'm serious. You're killing me. I can't write since I've been with you. I can barely get out of bed if you are next to me. Is this how you destroy a man?"

"Come off it. You are just paranoid and I don't want to hear one of your rants."

"See, you don't believe me that I have a real fear. I love you, but I don't trust you. Yes, I know you wouldn't cheat on me, but this living we are doing together is killing me."

"Well, I love you too."

"That was all I wanted to hear, thanks."

To Know and Understand

I told her I slept in a single-sized bed so we had to lie close to each other and cuddle, if that was okay with her.

"That is okay," she said.

She had long, shiny, obsidian hair that cut my face when she sat on top of me and leaned over to give a kiss. She had brown eyes that I lost myself in and cheekbones like mountains.

"I would've given you the horse I stole, but I had to eat it," I said.

She said, "I understand."

I was scared with her because I felt safe and after we had sex I said to her, "I should've told you when I first met you I have a terminal illness. It's painfully fatal."

"I know," she said. "I think you gave it to me. It's life and it's too beautiful to live or let down."

"I'm sorry," I said and rested my head on her chest. "I should've forewarned you, but I was selfish and I didn't want it to feel like a promise."

"I know," she said. "I understand."

Indian Woman

I want an Indian woman who is finished dying. I'm done wasting my time on women who idle in life. I want an Indian woman who wants to create two Indian children who love themselves. I want to say to my children, "We made you and you can change the future."

I want an Indian woman to say to me, "Let's not waste away. We are not headed up, but forward."

So far, my life hasn't existed. I live for what is beyond myself. I am alive and I can meagerly say I want an Indian woman who is not like me.

The Fingers

I have faith, it is with my fears, but I will enjoy this graceful moment, dive into its tranquility.

I kissed you to dissolve, sank under your blankets, and saw your beauty. I will hold my breath. I know silence.

I let my fingers feel your thighs and my legs relaxed. Now it's your turn to make the noise.

I watch you leave out the door and my loss with its cloak lifts to find me alone.

Tracing the Source

I am ready to hold the wooden brushes. I am drawing blueprints for your feet to trace, your sight to lust after. It is all yours; it was never mine, nor was it anyone else's deep night.

You and I will walk with the dead as we did with the living: both narrow to each other, but together frame-by-frame in every lashing hour. These right angles are fists that touch the same shores.

I held the night and the voice away from your temperament that evening. I was not insane. I was falling very slowly, and rose without silence. Call me crazy if I still talk to the walls, call tonight, but also listen and hear the music. It will lull the hum and you will sleep forever, and then sing with the traffic lumbering until the afternoon.

Here you sat and drank until your father called like a crow. Here you paced looking at your books, expecting them to leave you unsatisfied. You said much of who you were and wept every syllable of his face.

So, forget the long promises, give away the chains, they were never there unless you needed to stay put, come back to this hand, face, and body.

An American Indian Love in a Western Novel

She wasn't unique either in what she said or what she had between her legs.

She promised assimilation, termination, and civilization.

She preferred her Indian to sell her spirituality at dime bag prices.

She wanted her Indian drunk on whiskey, trying to ride a pale horse into a fiery sunset.

She wanted her Indian man to stay another night and not leave her and the kids like her father did with her mother.

She was half Indian and wanted me to ravish her, wildly break her innocence, then with her white half kill me: the savage warrior who tarnished her.

I Was Your Crazy Horse
(a sacred name that is not to be said aloud)

I came back to you often and asked if you still remembered those good, long nights, if we could build another fire, if we could drink only water. Did you remember the Indian, the horse, and the sad hour? Did you remember I was your Crazy Horse? Though you couldn't say it to my face. You couldn't remember the last Crazy Horse who wasn't afraid to stand near you. You said I was brave at the funeral, shoveling heavy, dry loads of earth. I didn't shed a tear.

You smelled my hair and worried about all the "ifs" before who stayed the night, worried if I would forget the aurora, the JD, the doorless outhouse. Forget the curve of laughter, the burn of motor oil, forget Crazy Horse was shaved bald by his own hand. He forgot he had other voices to sing along with, compete with, to silence. Did you remember I was your Crazy Horse, and you were afraid to say my name?

Motel Bed

If nothing comes, I am here next to your skin, neither fearing light
nor the lack thereof. I will not leave like a scar that was once a long cut
in your skin. I am here in your darkness, black as my hair and just as
brittle as your fingernails.

My heart pumps blood, lungs breathe air, body decays and replenishes.
Your white skin in dim light contains shadows like the thoughts I
have of love's hellhound licking my face. Am I living my secret life with
wounds that are desires, borne by loneliness?

I rest in a single bed at night under a green quilt, a blue and white star
quilt on the wall, nightlight on, stereo softly purring jazz. I am in bed
with another you. Afterwards in my arm crook they say my name. Here I
am without clothes as they are, to live with the fear of death. Am I dark
to them? Am I the man they wished to conquer, who is skin deep with
their silent fear?

To Play It Cool

In her bathroom I dry heaved above the porcelain until the bile flavored my tongue and my chest ached.

She knocked on the bathroom door. "What's wrong?" she asked. I flushed the toilet. I opened the door and there she stood. I scratched my head and gave a half-hearted smile.

She squinted her eyes. "It's not worth it," she said. "Have you been taking anything?"

"Two cans of beer a night before I sleep," I said. "And two pills I found in my drawer this afternoon, and solid foods every now and then."

She put her arms around me. We walked to the living room and sat on the futon couch. She touched my forearm. I jammed my hands into my pants pockets and fumbled with my keys. It's a guarantee a white woman will break a big Indian man's heart, but what hurts more is if it's an Indian woman.

Her head with its long black hair was snug in the hook of my right arm and with my left hand I played with her chest like an upright bass.

"Baby," I said. "You harmony and melody, you my music tonight before I go and fight with other poets. Before I go brawl over glass words and strong libations."

"From you," she said, "I don't want any expectations." She said this as I walked out the front door.

Broken Treaties

The promises she had in her voice were broken treaties. I wanted to believe her, but I've come across her lips before. Her words were with a slow careless precision of a redskin, a curl of forehead and matted hair tuft. Her woven melodies shrilled in my head. The promises she had in her voice were broken treaties. I wanted to believe her, but she had good intentions and I don't believe in good intentions.

The Visit

For Jamie "Chappie" C.

I sat on a bench below your kitchen window. I measured dry leaves, divided grass blades, rolled dirt between my fingers.

I drown in air, in green music, the seeds of clouds, hair strands, words on paper.

My arms flailed mixtures, oceans calmed, crows lined the roof, my eyes burned. I can't make a fist. Death would be easy now.

There where I sat again wanting to return to fingers that cleaned brown rice, to a kiss that stopped the blue world, to palms that measured salt, to a patched hole in the heart. I wanted to return to the stained touch and the sadness of your hands.

Matilda in Portland, Oregon

Matilda couldn't bend her right index finger, never could make a thumbs-up fist. But she would point her forefinger at me like a gun and drop her thumb. She was a quarter Indian and had hair like red flames turning in the sun and down the side of her face.

She had freckles on her body like maps to a secret room. My fingerprints would smudge on her chin as I drew her close for a kiss. She lay there in my single bed and I couldn't figure if she was beauty or death, or some other life that would freeze in summer dusk.

She was on her period when we had sex. Afterwards, I stood in the bathroom doorway as she squatted in the bathtub. I wanted something close to forever as she rinsed herself. She dried off and kissed me before she put on her denim skirt. It was like this the first time we ended our relationship the previous year.

Matilda's son was three years old when I first met him. He had dark hair, dark eyes, a nasally voice that talked with deep compassion. The last time I saw him he was five years old. We sang songs together and he asked if I wanted a beer, or if I was going to read poetry tonight. When he sat on my lap he said my hair smelled good, and do I remember the trading cards he said I bought him. I never bought them. I found them at a garage sale in a castle on the West Hills. Matilda paid for them.

But that was springtime and that was safety. Now, I stand on Broadway and Burnside wearing a shirt she gave me. It once belonged to her dead father. I walk the cold streets and hope not to see any resemblance of her, else a nervous fit would take over and I'd hide in a bar behind a rum and coke.

So far, I've been sick three weeks with fever and cough. I pass out every night without dreaming. I wake in a cold room, body fevered, half-empty beer cans next to the bed. I don't want to leave my room.

One Bad Night

This would be easier if you were dead, or worse, if we were married. It's okay, it was only a small scar, it was my steak knife anyways, that you threw, but I was right when I said your food that night tasted like shit.

Let's start the whole thing over. I'm willing to let bygones be bygones, all those women I had were nothing. After sex I couldn't stand them anyhow; their petty lives, or husbands, or nearly dead dogs, or their god damn cats.

"Three quarters white," you said. "That's why you're with me."

"If one-quarter Indian is good enough for the government," I said. "Then that's good enough for me, but that's not why I'm with you."

So here I am driving long nights, sipping beer, and sleeping in my car by an airport runway.

I want noise from the noise in my head. I'm making it daily to work, still not having enough sleep, still raging at nothing.

I prayed for lesions on my brain. I'm glad we didn't have children, else, all of this would be one bad night.

Mona Lisa's Smile

Mona Lisa was an Indian femme fatale. She wore the tightest black skirts, thin strapped high heels, smoked a pack of cigs a night. Her hair was long, jet black and shined in the shafts of moonlight.

Her dead father gave her the name. Her mother kicked Mona Lisa out when she was fifteen.

Mona Lisa got her own place, worked as a waitress at different greasy spoons until she was twenty-one then it was hole in the wall taverns. That's when I met her. She served me a rum and coke.

She said, "Because I could tell that's what you drank."

I asked for a cherry on top. She smiled and touched my hand.

I asked, "What do you want with a jerk like me?"

She said she had a lonely double bed and my suitcase looked more tired than me. I finished my sixth rum and coke at closing time. She hooked her arm in mine and we lived together for three years.

One morning in the kitchen we ate eggs and bacon, drank good bloody Marys. Afterward she brought me into the bedroom, kissed me, and put a gun to my head and said, "This is love. Baby, this is love. Now leave or you're dead."

I take the blame for fooling around with her best friend. But she wasn't worth keeping for more than an hour. I didn't care for her, but I'll do it again. Heck, she was a beautiful train wreck.

I never had the luck Mona Lisa had. In her eyes I was an empty parking lot, a cost not worth the space. I never wanted money, only a home, and left with 200 bucks on loan.

I left town with my dusty hat, suitcase, roll of toilet paper, and a plastic flower in a vase. I worked graveyard shift at a corner convenient store. I slept in a one-room motel with a shag-carpeted floor. Every morning I finished off two cold forties, read the funny papers, and smoked a pipe. Some afternoons I dreamed of Mona Lisa, of that collected once I could've made her cry, but she was stronger than I and didn't shed a tear, but showed a slight smile and gave a faint sigh.

Love

1.

I fell to my knees, raised my arms, hands opened to the Gorge and Columbia River. The shafts of sun pierced through clouds. The overcast disappeared and the river calmed.

Seagulls were like confetti thrown in the air. I am an idiot to say I know of love or let alone the divine. I am profane if I say I came to you to live. In the shadows I searched for your beauty. You said untruths and in them, I found strangled beauty. I requested death and you fed me light, stripped my clothes off, and chopped my body to bits. Now, I sit, wild-haired in bed then stand and scratch at the terror behind the walls. No more odes to madness or love through litanies. I haven't a word left to write. False love was had and I am finished.

2.

What the fuck do you know of love? You are scared of its steeds, the muscle, and bone. It is skinless marred of heart and wrapped in gold leaf. You're a cold heart of a creature with steel arms. This was you in your desire for oblivion.

I've seen in your eyes fear and heard the same from your tongue. Ice would be too warm for what you know of love. Living was not for daydreamers, remember, nor was love. You're just a half-life, green, and decayed.

Poems Not as Good as Money

I sat for hours in the chair she gave me.

She wanted money. I accepted this. I am a poet and poets never make enough money.

I sat and listened to two clocks compete for the right time.

I'll never have enough money to make a practical life: paid bills, nice furniture, all the things that made happiness for her.

I sat in the chair reading poetry. There will never be enough money. I am going into debt for poetry. She wanted money. I wanted poetry.

I sat in this chair for a while and wrote and read and pondered with a drink in hand. She wanted money and I am poet. The clocks ticked facing each other. I accepted I would never have enough money. Poetry has been there and will be until I sit again upright in my deathbed with words and lessened memories. She wanted money and I wrote penniless poems. I accepted this and each poem I write, I'll know she wanted money, but I only had poems.

Love and Hate Are in the Same Hand

They played us like cards. I knew I would never win, but I played because you were there. I threw down weak hands, closed my eyes. I expected you to go, but you never left. You sat next to this body. I hated you because I loved lies. I loved you because I hated your willingness to show truth.

I cheated to stay longer when you won. Don't deal me out. I will return with more funds. I will be there to see your hands take my money and watch secrets settle into the slow night.

I forgot you had your own life to attend, your own hand to lie down. My pair could never beat your full house. I can't trust my instincts. I should go before I see your next hand. They might win the war, but I lived for each struggle. I will be back to take you down.

Friends, Lovers

Angela was a red-headed single mother. She was my girlfriend then ex-girlfriend. Vicki was a Mexican single mother, a fair-weathered friend mostly. Well, I learned to keep her that way.

After Angela and I split, Vicki and Angela got together. I imagined them when their children were asleep, the two girls talking over wine, then in bed, rolling over each other, licking each other's parts, sweating and moaning, brown skin and white freckled skin, dark hair and red hair, entangling each other or some nights, when they needed a cock, an idiot skater kid would join in.

All my ex-girlfriends were bisexual. I thought I wouldn't have any concerns about my male friends, let alone the female ones, fucking my girlfriend.

Well, you got to choose very carefully your friends just like you have to choose with precision your lovers, especially if you are in love with them.

A year later I got back together with Angela. It ended again two months later. I'm neither friend nor stranger to Angela and Vicki or their kids, but some nights I let my cigarette burn to my fingers to feel what it's like when a friend fucks my girlfriend.

2

You fucking idiot, I'm not stoic,
this is just my face.

My Pony

In Portland my car doesn't speed more than she wants. Before I start her up or when she is purring or when she chugs between gearshifts, I say to myself, I think she's dying. But it's okay if she doesn't want to go faster than my desires.

In fact, I'm glad she is unable to quickly move. Especially when I had a long night of bar hopping and drunken love attempts and misshapen conversations. I drive home guided by my thumbs on each side of the steering wheel or drive with one eye open. I thank my car for bringing me home and while she sleeps in the parking lot behind my apartment, I hope every night after all my drunken nights driving in the rain, she may never give out.

Indian Spirit Guide

My ancient Indian spirit guide is the one to whom I listen. It's not my fault that my ancient Indian spirit guide is a boozehound with a gold, booze tooth in his smile.

Excerpt from the Diary of Sitting Bull

"One thing I fondly miss about George Armstrong Custer, besides the pretty, yellow locks bobbing up and down, were the splendid hand jobs. We would lie on long summer grass by the Little Big Horn River. You would be surprised how soft his hands were. Sure, he boasted a lot of shit, but at least he could live up to his namesake, Good-Hand-Job-Custer."

The Last Great Indian Casanova

She pulled away from our make-out session in the bar's restroom.

She asked, "Is that a tomahawk in your pants or are you just happy to see me?"

"It doesn't matter," I answered. "Baby, whatever it may be, it'll still split you like a log."

Zombie Love

She sat on the couch, mouth opened and doe-eyed. "I've met my father two or three times," I said.

She didn't say anything, but sat open-mouthed and doe-eyed. "I guess, now, I don't need a friend like that," I continued.

"I could do without a lot of stuff and that goes for people too. I guess I'm just like my father."

She didn't move, but sat mouth opened, doe-eyed, and snored. "Christ, she's a zombie," I said. "How the hell can I love a woman who sleeps with her eyes open?"

Add It Up

I'm a drunk Indian, which is very cliché.

I'm a dime-a-dozen guitar player, cliché too.

I'm a drunk Indian and a guitar player. I'm cliché squared. I write poetry, poets are a dime-a-dozen and very cliché.

I'm a cliché to the third power: a drunk Indian who plays guitar and writes poetry. Total worth: 1/6 of a dime.

Matchstick Tribe

This night I'm building houses out of wooden matches and people out of matchsticks. They are red faces wearing white hats with brown bodies.

The matchstick people are concerned that the houses are made of matchsticks. They stand back and look over the buildings, some fall to their knees and act out they are wiping away tears.

I light the buildings and a look of horror is in each of the matchstick people's eyes.

I bunch the matchstick people in a rubber band and set fire to their heads. There is no screaming.

Boredom

I was sitting in a bar with this sweet little girl. I was sipping a beer and rubbing my balls underneath the table. She rambled on about her mundane day. I watched her lips open and close. I licked my lips. I finished my beer and went to take a piss and when I came back she was gone, nowhere to be seen. I was relieved and ordered another beer. I was glad I didn't have to put up another front and pretend I wanted to hear more about her and her family. I abhor a bore.

Slam Poetry

1.
Slam poets talk like car salespeople because they're as good as processed meat, as clever as pop culture, and as ironic as a soup can.

2.
With slam poetry, another thing I hate is it goes on and on. The slam poet should truly edit their poem to be as concise as they can without sounding like an electric fan buzz. I like my poetry the way I like my pussy and that is tight.

Birthday Party Sweater

She had a beer goggle beauty that only an alcoholic could appreciate. She talked of her family problems, newborn children, or who was doing what.

She leaned in close and said she liked my smell. I said to her I like the way her nipples poked out from underneath her sweater.

I took a pull on my beer. She crossed her arms and covered her tits. Her sweater fitted her real good.

Secondhand Underwear

At the thrift store, I rummaged through the lingerie section. I wanted to buy my girlfriend something for her birthday and money was an object. It would be funny, I thought, if I bought my girlfriend a lingerie outfit from the thrift store.

Of course, she would disapprove because it was second-hand underwear, but firstly because it was tacky.

What other love has happened in here? I thought, examining a black nightie. I looked around the store and judged by the vehicles parked in front, S.U.V.s and station wagons, that they were soccer moms who walked about.

I held up another possible garment and wanted to smell it.

"I better not," I said aloud, then thought, people might think I was a cheap Casanova, but firstly think I was a pervert.

I placed the clothing back on the rack and felt the fabric of other garments.

If I was to buy something like this, I thought, eventually it will return to another second-hand store. I didn't think love was that kind of recyclable, or at least I didn't want to think it was.

I walked past soccer moms with their kids as I left the store. Love was recyclable, I thought, it better damn well be reusable. It better be durable like a callus else it wouldn't be worth the time to make it.

John Wayne Instinct

When I think of America and cowboys, I think of John Wayne. John Wayne walked with a holier-than-thou attitude, he talked with authority, he killed passionately. John Wayne portrayed characters in movies of every noble idea that made America's arrogance.

Just the sound of his voice and you knew America was in the room. If you were brown, a streak of fear would overcome you. If you didn't speak English you could guarantee to be a dead man, a dead culture.

John Wayne lived by his gut instinct. He exuded who he was from his gut. John Wayne died with 60 pounds of impacted feces in his gut. Much like America, John Wayne, in his characters and ideas, was full of shit.

Real Indian Junk Jewelry

You have probably seen them at pow wows. They would wear absurd
amounts of turquoise. They would have a huge turquoise rock on a belt
buckle or on a ring. Maybe have some on a bracelet, necklace, a pair
of earrings. Some would go as far as to have a turquoise eye instead
of a glass one or when they smiled, a full grill of turquoise rocks.
TURQOUISE: the Indian bling-bling.

What's Your Background?

June, who was drunker than the rest of us, brought this guy, Mark, who, Dick, Joseph, and I didn't know. Before Mark asked his question, we all introduced ourselves. I shook my head at June because I knew this fucker was an idiot.

Mark was brought over to our table because June said she wanted an experiment, which would conclude men were bastards. In her experiment she walked up to random men in the bar, talked, and then made out with them. Sure, any guy would make out with an attractive woman in a bar if both were drunk. There wasn't any real experiment, only horny men wanting to lay their seed in a hole.

"What's your background?" Mark asked me.

Since I'm a six-foot-one, 240-pound Lakota man, and looked the part of an Indian (long, black hair in ponytail, mountainous cheekbones, and brown skin), every idiot thinks it important to ask my ethnicity.

I gritted my teeth and squinted my eyes.

"My friend, Joseph, here to my right," I said. "Is a European mutt and next to him is an Irish/Scott piece of shit. June here is German, mostly, and I am Pre-American."

I don't remember what Mark said, but I remembered I said pointing my right index finger at him, "Why don't you move on, asshole, else I'll slice your throat and call it manifest destiny, rip out your heart, and call it Wounded Knee. GET THE FUCK OUT OF MY FACE GEORGE ARMSTRONG CUSTER!"

Mark stood and left the table leaving his beer behind. We all laughed except for June.

"You're an asshole," she said.

"Yeah, but he's an idiot," I said. "And he should not be shown any mercy."

Men are idiots for a cunt and would be willing to follow a piece of ass into the flames of hell. A woman's hole is only an open grave and clit, a tombstone. They are a bad gateway drug. So I treat them as such. June left the table and went outside to talk on her cell phone. After a few minutes I followed.

"All he wanted to do was fuck your hole," I said. "Men are pieces of shit."

"You bastard," she said.

"Valid statement, but I'm looking after your well-being. I have to put the situation in this light so you can retain some information from tonight."

"Fuck you. I'm not one of your idiots."

"None of this matters. It doesn't mean to make any sense."

She didn't say anything and pulled me close and we kissed.

3

Happiness is uncomfortable.
You know,
it's that glowing sensation in the chest.
I have to maintain myself at
an even emotional level.
If I'm too happy
I would crash hard. If I'm depressed
it will all get worse.

Let Them Rage

I can't remember names let alone yesterday, maybe it never happened,
and tomorrow is wishful thinking.

At dawn the starlings can sing without me. I'm tired of mourning.
I'll let it go with the ghosts who will visit tonight.

Let them rage, let them sit in rocking chairs, rock and meditate.

I'm retiring to the soil's mouth. Let her kiss and devour this sod.

Again the Air was Thin

Again the air was thin. I cried the blues and have sown the nights together. Again smoke filled the room, I cried the blues and pushed away from shores. Again there was an unbearable doorway from where I cried the blues and covered the wounds. Again it stopped my breath these blues I would cry, these blues I cried. Again you walked out and I cried the blues.

O Lord, have I lived a wonderful life? O Lord, forgive the snow, and fire, and Lord, O I bled and cried the blues.

Before Turning 27

In a couple of days I'll drink poison, stand in the ocean barefoot with every element of life: fire, dirt, wind, and water. I could be wrong, but I know it'll make sense later: a good woman can turn a good man bad.

Portland Lights

Somewhere between the earth and sky, just over the horizon where the fallen sun died. I looked at the city. Each streetlight was a word, and the city itself, a flickered poem.

This is Where I Grew and Lived

Yes, this is where I placed your favorite book, on my shelf to gather with dust.

This is where I placed the last picture I took of you when your face reminded me of a poem I couldn't quite remember, but it was one I had put to memory.

This was the music I neglected. It was the atmosphere I captured and in it was made to wander alone.

This was the life I played like an out-of-tune violin or a guitar that couldn't hold its strings.

I looked over my room and tried to put meaning to objects. This was my longing.

Street Ghosts

Each gunshot was an angel who cawed for the first time. In my neighborhood, every new ghost walked by my window. I nodded to them and the dogs barked from across the street.

The ghosts were in fear and ran screaming under the streetlights.

I have seen ghosts jump at my window. I had to tell them to move on. Some listened and some continued to run.

I left food on the back porch, this was to let them know they were thought of and they should continue on their journey.

When I sat drunk on my living room couch, they took advantage of me and danced on the coffee table. I would laugh at them, but they stood there and screamed. They touched my face and then disappeared.

Gunshots were every other night, dogs barked every hour, the nights were heavy with ghosts who wanted me to know them.

Lorca and I

I found a book by Lorca in the public library. The pages were torn out. Someday the book will be mended, but not by me. I leave the book on the floor with the pages next to hard cover like its heart next to body; a small body that might by others be looked over.

I lay down next to the leaf stacks. My heart was torn out like the promises of possibility and always.

These words are yellow flowers coloring a decomposed body. Those who find me let them radiate. I have lived well and never had regret.

My Lover, Death

Death, you are not worth your prize. Remove the blankets, burn the pages that spoke of liberty.

I've missed you, friend. You have come to my cell for a visit either bewildered by the meaning or tamed by its idea of life.

Death, I welcome you back, though I have lost the blighted belief of rest. Seize with me the hunger, the feast of lions. We swept the dust off each other.

I choose you to say my last speeches. Leave me alone to the frail leaves underneath your steps then drink my wandered love in the night.

It must be this way. I am ash. I request again to remove the flames you set in me.

The Rusted, Red Wheelbarrow

If it was joy or sorrow, sunshine or rain it didn't matter. We still smoked hand-rolled cigarettes and drank potato moonshine beside a faded barn or on a wooden bench overlooking a harvested cornfield. We used it to haul our drunken bodies back to the small farmhouse or had it for our foodless vomit.

This is why so much depended upon the rusted, red wheelbarrow filled with more weight than the head can carry.

The Writing Process

They come out of the walls. I can make out their hands, read their faces.
The insanity of their stories makes sense.

Here is the future in memory: ex-lovers, lost friends, long drives to the
Pacific, a beach fire, coughing on smoke, a silent lighthouse.

It is a belief that nobody would crash the rocks or have a fear of home.
They are the journeys in whiskey shots in white rooms.

Meditation

I light a stale Cuban cigar, sip my third forty. I am done with the fight. Tonight I will unnaturally rest early. The last page is torn out. I laid my fork down. The feast is finished. The horses lick my bones. I gave up years before. I have let the firewater world consume and suffocate the parts of me that couldn't be repaired.

Truths

I have never cursed myself by chasing a dream. I don't believe in the ephemeral. I live and what is laid before me is what I rummage through. I'm all action without the pretense alluded through words.

What is important are the cold facts, the setting, and the personal work I do now. Nice people will always be nice. I don't want nice. I want direct action because I can count on it. Sincerity only goes as far as one is able to give, honesty only comes out of what is dishonest. A liar is nothing and I don't care enough for this world to say I want to fight for a better one.

There are too many facts, but as the old poets say, truth is beauty. It doesn't matter if it's as ugly as money or as beautiful as a F.A.S. child. I can depend on my hands to write, my brain to think, and my life to end.

Who Else Has Been Here

I am in a small single room of an old motel on a street corner in
Pendleton, Oregon.

I sit at a table snug against a wall and look at the bed I am to sleep
in tonight.

The comforter laid across the bed has probably been washed more times
than I want to imagine.

Someone, I bet, sat on the edge of the bed and talked on the phone
while they saw themselves in the mirror behind the small color T.V.

They'd mention the dry heat, the sun disappearing its glow behind Mt.
Hood, but never mentioned missing someone.

Then I look out the window at the kidney bean shaped pool aglow by
a streetlight.

I wish this were all new.

I close the curtains, pull off the comforter, cover myself in the bed
sheet, and listen to the air conditioner rattle from its perch in the
back window.

Somebody in the next room coughs, outside cars drive by, and with the
lights left on, I close my eyes and sleep.

Neruda

In this dream I was buying beer and at the newspaper stand there was a poetry magazine. I picked it up and opened it to the middle. There was a Neruda poem printed and on the opposite page was one of mine, then the scene changed.

I was in bed with a woman. We were having sex at her place. The beer I bought earlier, I drank it all and I was thinking I should be having fun, I should be enjoying this, but I knew differently. I was used and she was too. We had sex for hours, but I just wanted to sleep in my own bed at home, alone.

When I'm drunk, dreams are difficult to separate from waking state. I didn't want any of this, I'm not a breeder. I'm tired of being a man.

Old Man 27

With dirt underneath my fingernails, I sit on my front stoop and sip beer. The radio plays jazz. The music fills the living room, spills out the windows, and open front door. My hands shake, sight is blurred, spine is killing me. I smoke a stale cigar, it is early afternoon and I fear DTs. In these times, I think about her and them and where I am. I keep my eyes closed longer, each blink burns. I don't want to exist, but I am damn sure I don't want to disappear. I open my eyes, my flesh, hands, bones, heart, brain. They've failed me more than people. My life is in each open bottle, in each dead little beast my cat paws on the sidewalk. Fuck, there ain't no love when death is scraping my skull, only rum and cokes from noon on. These days I am wandering between streetlights after sundown, and tilling hard, cold earth. I am removing rocks that were once people.

Wedding Music

At my friends' wedding in Manzanita, Oregon, he recited a poem to her written by Billy Collins.

This is how I would like my wedding to be, but also include Bukowski, Neruda, and Rumi.

To hear the break of the blue word by the ocean is music enough. Ah, simple magic. Forget the wedding. I want this every night.

When It Finally Comes

I drink my last 2 dollars. I cock my head back, look for the stars, lean back a long pull from a forty-ounce heaven. I'm never broke when I sip the last greatest beer. I sip it like gnawing on a bullet. It tastes like my last hour on earth. Beautiful.

What They Wanted

Does one wonder while stirring green tea if to be alone was lonely or how does one recognize a loss when one isn't lonely, though they are alone? It was through madness that I contemplated such a placid view. I believed I walked with everything or calloused my fists to the stale walls. It wasn't in loss that I moved this way; it was a night when I didn't want rest. I watched the rain like wet sunlight bounce tree limbs and turn leaves around. I have changed this loneliness. I replaced its sounds with emptiness and in it I lived in denial. I got by and that was what everyone wanted really.

4

Family is murder. They grow you
and expect you to be sane,
but what flourishes are the constant
chipping off
of your endurance, mind,
and spirit. Damn,
if I could do it all over again I wouldn't
do anything at all.

The Old Moan

The old moan of man, moan of the old, of the reflections in a cracked mirror blurred by smoke damage. Play your blues tonight, man. Play and groan, I know your songs by heart and I have lived them beside you. I have pushed in the darkened liquid deep through my veins. I untied the ribbon wrapped around the upper arm. I felt history sag further in me. Moan, of love, of loss, grief and happiness, of the loud and tranquil, of the emptiness kept in the silence between phrases of your melody. Alone, moan and groan the blues where nothing is kept sacred. Sell the one soul we have, let the leaves shake and the night drip like moonlight rain. Our halos are rusted, our throats are sore, eyes no mo' cry and the homes we left are those great street signs that ask, but never demand.

O my baby ain't ever comin' home. O my baby ain't never comin' back. She took the keys, left me on my knees, said I was never a fact. The old moan of man. Moan, moan, moan.

Fear's Endurance

1.

My mother in one of her blackouts called me a fag and cried about how grandfather had her stand on the kitchen table and dance, grandfather with a bullwhip in hand lashed her with the tears she now cried.

I didn't want to be born, they had to pull me out of my mother and since then I cursed her for birthing me out of her loneliness.

For the longest time I didn't like to take showers. I remembered baths only. I never liked what showers hid from loved ones. My mother hid herself in a shower and I still hear her sobbing.

2.

Once I pissed into my grandfather's wine bottle. I wanted him to stop drinking. I remembered his smell was cheap wine, beer, Pall Malls.

My grandfather pushed a shopping cart through the streets of San Jose, CA, and with his friends drank and camped off the side of a road, deep in golden brush.

He taught the Lakota language to friends, never to his children or his grandchildren. The times I heard my language spoken was from him with the stink of cheap beer on his breath.

When he wasn't drunk, he was a burden. He'd sit at the kitchen table and read the newspaper, tear strips from it and eat it. This was after a day of going through withdrawal, with muscles cramping and family rubbing his body.

3.

I write this now, drinking a half-empty bottle, and have been drunk for 6 months straight. I fell off a wagon I never knew I was on.

Here, on this planet I am Indian first, human second, and still an Indian last. I can't remember pow wow melodies and my grandfather is dead.

I can't claim a reservation because I matured in a city and if I see on the concrete streets another Indian walking toward me, I make sure not to make eye contact or else walk another direction.

My one fear is when I'm dead would I need to know my language to journey to the spirit world, will the dead forgive my youth, will they not let me down as I had with others.

Death is my one guarantee for the price of life. I figure that each day is close enough for a good day to die.

Intertribal Street

1.

The last pow wow I attended was a New Year's pow wow in the Portland Armory. An owl dance was announced and a girl asked me to dance. I turned her down.

As was the rule I had to give her money and apologize, I didn't. I sat in a gray folding chair as the announcer pointed in my direction. Everyone looked my direction, but I wasn't ashamed.

"I don't have any money," I yelled. "I'm an Indian man without his language and land."

Everyone nodded in agreement and I shook my head.

I thought as I sat there of why the girl asked me to dance. She might have wanted love. She might have wanted Indian children. She might have wanted happiness. She might have wanted to save an Indian man without his language and without a home.

2.

That was the last time I attempted murder with a big, cheap bottle of red wine and three boxes of sleeping pills.

A year later in the south park blocks a friend said an Indian writer killed himself in the J.F.K. airport.

I thanked her for the information. She walked on and I sat on a bench. I let the hot tears roll down my cold face.

I'm sorry my friends if I scared you, but I was scared myself.

3.

A Northwest Indian complained about Plains Indians who have migrated to his Northwest.

In my case I told him I came to destroy myself and have my ashes thrown into the Pacific Ocean.

He looked at me without saying a word and walked away.

4.

I sat with a lady friend in a corner café. A Lakota elder saw me through the front window. He came into the café and asked to talk with me outside.

The elder said he didn't like the idea of an Indian man who was friends with a white woman. Then he asked if he could borrow a couple of dollars.

"Love is hard to find with any person," I said to him. "You got to think of your people," he said.

"That's my problem. I can't stop thinking of my people. It's my people who make me think of my people."

"You urban Indians are all the same."

"Thank you, I needed the validation from an elder asshole."

He looked at me mean and grabbed the dollar from my hand and walked off.

My lady friend paid for the coffee. We left the café and went back to her place and drank wine and made love on the couch, then in the bathroom, and finally on her bed.

Blood on the Basket

Lucien was five years old. His mother, Carolyn, and he were at a convenience store in the next town off the reservation. He looked at the ground from the blue pickup truck window, he saw the light, brown, dirt road surrounding the trailer home turned corner store. Carolyn walked out of the store with a couple of beer cases, six-pack of half sized soda cans, and a bag of nacho-flavored chips.

Lucien struggled to pull the tab off the soda can. "Do you need some help?" Carolyn asked.

"No Ina, I can do it," Lucien answered.

Carolyn put on her favorite country western tape in the tape player that lay between her and Lucien. The truck quickly pulled out of the parking lot. A cloud of brown dust engulfed the pickup as it drove onto the paved highway.

The summer sun drifted down the horizon. Bales of hay, which sat across a stretch of green plains, glowed golden with wisps of purple. After eating half the bag of chips and finishing two sodas, Lucien closed his eyes and was lulled to sleep by the hum and low rumble of the truck. Carolyn turned off the tape player.

Lucien's earliest memories of living on the reservation were mostly unpaved roads that led to each of his families' H.U.D. houses. He lived with his mother, aunt, and cousins in a two-bedroom H.U.D. house. Lucien and his mother slept in the basement and shared an unframed double bed on the cement floor.

There was a party in progress when Lucien and his mother arrived home. One of Lucien's aunts carried him from the truck to the basement bed, took off his shoes, and tucked him in bed. The aunt passed her hand across Lucien's round face, down his chest and stopped above his heart. She felt the rise and fall of Lucien's chest. She continued down his stomach and circled around Lucien's crotch. Lucien rolled to his side and the aunt stood and went back up stairs.

Loud pounding and yelling startled Lucien from his dream of flying over the Black Hills. He ran up the stairs in the dark, opened the basement door, and ran through the kitchen to the hallway before the bathroom. His aunts were pounding on the locked bathroom door.

"Open this door right now, Carolyn!" one of Lucien's aunts demanded.

"No! No! Leave me alone! I don't want to live!" Lucien's mother screamed.

The sound of his mother crying and the pounding of fists thundered in Lucien's ears. He ran through the hall calling for his mother.

One of the aunts kicked open the bathroom door and Lucien saw his mother sprawled on the floor. Blood was sprayed across the walls and white tiled floor. Carolyn looked up at her sisters with blood on her face and cried louder.

An aunt picked up Lucien and carried him to the living room. Lucien pressed his face into his aunt's chest as they sat on the couch and sobbed.

The Ways of Medicine

George Medicine removed the tenor sax from his mouth after one long, forlorn tone. Some of the audience in the Flat Nickel Jazz Club wept, some were silent, and some sipped their drinks. The bass player's fat forefinger pedaled the strings of his upright bass while George stood with his head raised in praise, eyes closed, lip tucked. When he lowered his head sweat-tears raced then fell from his face.

George Medicine put the sax back into his mouth and started to finger the muse in a flow of deep, blue notes. He continued a condensed life moan in each breath. Each turn in the melody fell out of the sax like bones turned to dust.

The drummer's brushes cautiously crossed the snare head and swept the rhythm holding all the musicians together.

They shuddered in repose. George wiped sweat from forehead, paced in his moccasins while the piano chords transcended with the stars outside. The musicians were down deep in their mantras.

I was in back of the club and leaned my head against the wall. I sipped my whiskey with each breath in George's melodies. I let the musical rapture stream in my body. It was an electricity of fear, anger, passion, the unknown unraveling. I then realized my breathing and stumbled through the oxygen-smoke that filled each booth puffed from Indians hip to George Medicine.

From behind dark sunglasses George looked around at the 1am crowd. He motioned a cadence to the song. The musicians relaxed their brain juices as the silence swallowed us. A quick two-beat count-off and they were gone to "A Night in Tunisia."

I settled for a quick walk around the block to get some fresh air and to score George some more dope. I looked around Old Town. I saw gum stains on the sidewalk like scars, like a language I was to figure out some night.

This was the morning, prayer dance with liquid jazz shooting through my head. The city streetlights yellowed on the street curbs. I walked and thought of George's tattered moccasins ruminating with each step made as they tapped the floor with tired toes. They tried to grab earth, to reassure that he was still on the ground.

A quick make down Burnside Street, past a crackhead suckling a glass tube. I came to a bridge and walked down some stairs and under the bridge, I saw a fellow Skin asleep in a hallowed doorway. He was cocooned with friends in damp sleeping bags. I had met him before, but not his gang. Whenever I ran into him we would talk about poems we carried in our breast pockets or the next Sundance or our loves lost by back store dumpsters. I carefully slipped a couple of bills in his sleeping bag with a handwritten note of hello and general good will. He automatically whispered, "thank you."

I headed back to the club through the purple moon-lit streets milled with red-eyed blues rushing through my body. I was back to the shadow of people in the smoky club. I saw George sway with the ride cymbal and smile at the girl in the front row with red ringlet hair. George had a lush swarm overcome him and he flexed his forearm with an A.I.M. tattoo, it glistened with his moaning body.

George had eyes of music and deep passion like a sentient melody drifting through his lungs longing for a love wasted by the weathered hard years. George was a worn man in a disappearing phrase. He closed the jazz chorus with a yell in ruptured perfection.

George Finds Medicine

George picked up his tenor sax, wetted the reed, fingered the possible songs, breathed deeply then placed the sax on his couch. He looked over the wear on the instrument. There were a few dents, a lot of scratches from nights of loss. He picked up the sax again and brought the chewed mouthpiece to his lips, breathed deeply, closed his eyes and thought of his father weeping on a couch. George blew into the sax and freed a tone.

His father was a large Lakota man, drunk, awash in vacant bottles. George as a child broke open one of the bottles. He wanted to wander the insides, to see why it carried his father's tears.

George connected a string of notes, whittled a melody, felt the song's changes underneath the angular lines. He played a genocide chant for an early morning massacre and stamped his bare feet on hot snow. George set fire to all his failures, grunted when he saw flesh melt under a storm of bullets. His passion smelled like burning music and sounded like screaming red voices.

The salt of weeping tasted like sweat from a yellow moon. Every woman he had loved and saw leave were rung from the few stands of white sounds. His hands ached as every finger touched each ghost that danced around him. His heart was a thunder sounded from a taut drum in a Sundance heat. One pulse was a rip of talons from his chest, another pulse was burnt flesh that birthed scars.

George's closed eyes saw all.

He inhaled and exhaled the blue vowels rasped from the sax. It was a song resembling blood or bones aged in the sun. George sat next to his father, felt his hunger, waited to turn the day into hope, a tomorrow into possibility. Sweet incense scorched his lungs with black tar. George bit through another reed and squealed in a train wreck.

Deer Soup, Fry Bread, Wojape

I stood in the Rez chow line waiting for a deer soup, fry bread, and *wojape* dinner.

I ate the chow line food on the hood of my car. I looked at the star-filled night across the cold South Dakota sky.

I counted all the stars that would take me home, saw every star that I knew would break my heart, every light speck that would never love.

I slept in a damp sleeping bag on a small, grass-patched field.

I woke the next day in the afternoon sun to the sound of drums. Drums like laughter, drums like crying, drums like empty beer cans, drums like old blankets, like old voices in new bodies.

I puked last night's meal on the shiny, yellow grass. I turned over and slept through the noise.

Manifest Bus Destination

I was never a warrior and there ain't nothing if you're an urban Indian, only the hate of a city, the American hunger for identity, and the defeat of no resolution. Nothing. I never learned a death song. I am in limbo.

We urban Indians pushed shopping carts half empty with rubber tomahawks and toy war bonnets with silly colored feathers. Our women are tribally made sterile by I.H.S. butchers, our elders rot in nursing homes.

Sometimes I felt like grave-robbed bones in the Smithsonian museum, waiting for family to pick me up like I was at a Greyhound bus stop, still waiting passed out with white man dreams of transfiguration.

Sometimes I felt like a corpse on display, alone, behind glass in a fictional scene. I was just more scenery. They said I was a great hunter, but in this scene I was only another object.

I was past tense in history books, a paragraph wide. They said I was a warrior, but now I'm mostly water, a few cells, and lost without a tongue. My scalp was bounty for the same price as a pound of Tillamook cheese.

Identities in two-dimensional mascot profiles speak broken languages. This is American honor.

True when you're an Indian there is always a war to fight.

(The smell of puke, piss, booze, and moldy sex surrounded me as I wrote this litany. I scratched this on a bus driving up a hill in a drizzle with other passengers looking forward, but only able to see as far as a dilapidated city block.)

Four Ways of Looking at a Red Cowboy

1.

His brown, wrinkled hand grips the collar of fortified wine in a green bottle. He loosens the yellow liquid down his throat. The surrounding noise dampens and any sign of hurt is lulled with weakened eyes. His dirty, western shirt lies on his belongings in a shopping cart cage. He teaches his language to his buddies, his family only hears a strange voice.

2.

His body cramps as the blue darkens around him. There is no money for booze so the edges are sharp again. The sun is brighter in this way. His blood is fire. He sweats in his cowboy boots with cardboard insoles. He pulls on his braids as a priest had done the first time he went to boarding school. They pulled his hair just before cutting it off. He was miles from family, lifetimes from home. He huddled with the rest of the nobodies around him.

3.

He woke before dawn with father and mother. They kneeled outside, prayed and thanked for seeing another day. He labored with relations in the dry, white sun. His red hand-made-to-fit ribbon shirt soaked in his sweat. His cowboy hat covered his dreams of riding broncs at a pow wow/rodeo. His small hands threw rope; he was green in his mistakes. He was told not to be Indian. He stroked an orange flame from kitchen matches and smoked Pall Malls.

4.

He lay in a dark closet watching the light from cars out the window race across the opposite wall. The lights were chasing existing shadows. The car noises were like water churning every few seconds. He turned over and slept with face muffled in a pillow. He sensed his dead wife in gathered scents. His brown, thin sleeping bag itched his legs. He feared small pox, but was wishing for it. He slept. He was home.

Becoming a Good End

Indian boy took his first drink. He tasted sweat from fear, blood from fear. The hot liquid burned his throat blue.

Indian boy was counting coup with each sip: this one for a father who was not around and this for a mother barely alive in a hospital.

Indian boy stole his first girl. She was a Jingle Dress dancer. He didn't see a face and didn't remember a name. He left her with a Pendleton blanket rash and love bruises on his neck.

The sour water in a warm brown bottle pounded his head with sad joy. The slow glasses crashed, broke the day, hit the floor, blinded the light, opened history. A music's hum in an Indian bar woke him to hidden tumbles as white as the fire of an aurora moon. It turned him to ash. Led him to who he was in a city's flame.

Indian boy felt like an absent man making promises on toilet paper treaties. They were only words, but they made worlds.

Indian boy stole his first pony. The loud grind of gears, the race of his heart, the feel of the steering wheel on impact.

Indian boy sleeps in his first grave after an all-night wake, the sweet smell in a multicultural center, songs of a drum group, and six feet of labored earth.

No, no.

Indian boy is fully grown. He is a man in the bind of life, a father of three possibilities. His wife has a beautiful face, her name is Suzy Gots-The-Gun, she no longer dances Jingle Dress, no, she is a Traditional Dancer. They live to see great-grandchildren run with fire and dance with water.

Work Is Finished

An Indian man, that's who I see on a TV monitor in my neighborhood corner convenience store. He's buying two PBR forties for the night, one to wash away despair and the other to wash away hope. He buys eight chicken nuggets with BBQ sauce to eat for strength, a cheap cigar to think it through when he sits on his tenement's back porch. He's 27 years old, it's 5pm and he's ready. I could see it in his eyes, in his lumbering walk. There's not much left to do but call it a day. He walks home with his evening under his arm in a brown paper bag. It's a humid five-block walk home. Today, the barking dogs are silent, crows are raggedly perched on tree branches, laughing kids run by, noise of car stereos comes and goes. Outside his tenement, a white cat lays in the middle of the road. Across the street, soul music blasts from a church. Some days he wants to burn it down, but today it feels pleasant.

Dancers

1.

I'm your Grass Dancer flattening grass of the arbor to dance all night.

I'm your Fancy Dancer. I move at the speed of light, and like the night, dazzle with stars.

I'm your Traditional Dancer, meditative and forever.

2.

There's always time anywhere for a slow dance, that moment when the world dims, joy and sorrow blend. There's always time to slow dance, always time to dissolve.

3.

If I close my eyes in the barroom smoke of our ceremony, I will fall. If I keep my eyes open, I will fall. If I look into your eyes, I will fall. I can say this now; I never take my own advice.

You pulled me aside, tugged my hair, kissed my lip, said, "I will fall too."

4.

She said, "I'm your Traditional Dancer, meditative and forever.

"I'm your Jingle Dress dancer, hear my body, you are alive. I'm your Fancy Shawl dancer.

We are out of the slumber where we've kept company in its cocoon."

5.
Under a table there's a puddle of beer, on the tabletop, a half-empty
glass, and in my hand a scribbled note.

This curled rice paper heart with holes. You stick your finger in and
redirect its flow. There is music everywhere.

6.
Owl Dance.

She held my hand and we moved. "Magic," she said. "I know the radiant
unknown, the swimming slivers under the skin, and what we are,
is magic."

Bus Stop

Moses Blood Lightning stood under a bus shelter and watched faces of young and old walk by him. He saw each face in all their various life stresses depart and arrive.

He looked up and saw his face's reflection in the bus shelter's glass ceiling. There were no evening stars especially in the meat of a city, but there was no need to look up anyhow, eye level was best.

He looked at the brick sidewalk, saw it shine from streetlights. It was a night after a sweep of light rain.

The buses' low vibratos shook him. Screaming metal brakes cracked the upper decibels, and passengers yawned in a silent choir.

Headlights were like apparitions of his past. They stopped at the curb or traveled on out of view.

A group of women laughed from his left, then in front of him, then to his right and back to the city noises.

Moses eyed some, but none held his interest. He walked to a T.V. monitor that showed the bus schedule and studied it. He was waiting for the number eight. He walked to a nearby, oddly-shaped fountain and watched water go from separation to reunion. None of it was drinkable liquid. He listened to the water splash and watched the sparkle of its music.

Most bus shelters had a bench to sit on, only for sitting. The bench was divided in two by a half looped bar, so no person could lie stretched and dream. Three glass walls were usually scratched by someone's frustration to be remembered and if they were forgotten, they might vanish.

There were no glass walls to hide from a wind. No benches to sit on under the glass canopy at Moses' bus stop shelter downtown by the university.

His stop was uninviting and temporary like all the conversations he had with people. They were here for their time, then dissolved to his memory's tattered envelopes.

Moses looked up again at his aged face. He still waited for tangible objects to stay for more than their welcome.

I Am in the Reservation of My Mind

I saw the best lives of my reservation destroyed by manifest destiny, hungered in commodity lines, passed out in broke down cars eight hours until the gas was gone and froze in a South Dakota snow storm.

Who inhaled lines of meth driving along empty HWYS, believed in American dreams, held cigars and turned to wood, looked at America again and turned to a salt pillar.

Who roamed the streets reeking of piss and sucked cock for crack, raped their sons in a drunken loneliness, prostituted their cousin in Pasco, Oregon for shots of H.

Who in asylums, received electroshock, sang death songs learned and understood only by the deceased.

Who were stolen, shaved, taken to boarding schools, screamed with angels and broke their bones, cut rivers into their wrist, searched for solace in the yellow-crusted moon.

Who constructed intricate nooses, wrapped them around their necks and swung in H.U.D. house basements.

Who were adopted children, slept on bus benches like angry birds and wandered in who they thought they were. Who were sterilized by I.H.S., born F.A.S., sat before the penumbra of TV commercials, lost their sight and feet to diabetes.

Whose hearts were crushed at Wounded Knee, obliterated by Mt. Rushmore, demonized by Crazy Horse Monument.

Who knelt before the cross, ate the flesh, drank the blood, were raped by catholic priests, recited a thousand by a thousand Hail Marys for every sin that shined like a blanket of stars as warm as small pox and as cold as biblical heaven.

Who carried a photo of George Armstrong Custer, raged a curse at the photo, held their sick buddy under the Burnside Bridge, drank can after can of Lysol.

Who huffed gasoline-soaked rags, laughed in the Portland streets, cut their long black hair by the radioactive glow of salmon.

Who were gunned down driving into the American dream, beaten to death for talking their language, burned alive for the word of god.

Who looked down, untied to girders 60 stories above Portland, New York, Seattle, San Francisco, San Jose, Los Angeles, looked down at busy ants building big, meaningless, abstract rooms.

Who didn't care anymore after mother's death, pulled out their eyelashes, dug their fingernails into their scarred legs, sat in a coma of gold cobwebs that wove their arms to the sun hidden behind thick clouds.

Who threw themselves into fiery lakes of literature, Harjo, Alexie, Ortiz, Welch, Momaday, Louis.

Who stood in faith on a different bridge every night, threw pill bottles into the Willamette River, cursed their hands' dependability, ate newspaper strips, sipped every inked character with their head lost in the streetlight music, strolled back to city park campsites.

Who said they were Crazy Horse or Jesus or Sitting Bull or Judas or Chief Big Foot, signed their life to the white noise of history burned on every page ripped out from the book of longing.

Who stole horses, called it freedom, leaned against padded rooms filled with wild horses strewn with sinewy strands of madness, rattled the cages, screamed from the rusted bars.

Who raged on top of Bear Butte, fucked next to each Black Hills tree, scratched ghostly promises of love written under blue moonlight on purple pages.

Who ran with the hunted, fell with the game, ripped skin from bone, listened to the ravished drums hidden in the chest, their hearts drilled by worms.

Who drove half-alive cars into riverbanks, smoked dope on sun-drenched cliffs, drew knives into naked arms, injected cooked jazz records.

Who walked thousands of miles to Oklahoma with deep pools of oblivion in their eyes, saw the absence of seven generations set among crooked trees, drowned in starvation.

Who were hanged with Dakota warriors at the hand of Abraham Lincoln, dared to say they were the dreams Crazy Horse had when he envisioned the future.

Who swam in the black between stars behind tarpaper houses, ripped talons from their chest, wept before the torn-down Sundance tree.

Who mended stolen skulls in museums, angrily searched for pieces of the hoop, found severed breast, dead Indian child, neglected elder, crazy horse dreams in Big Chief notebook.

Who clawed the earth heart for rocks of gold, drank to remember the contour of a circle, insanely danced into the hollowed songs of loss, elated in sweat and paper promises, believed in the safety words created, tore free their heart from the chest of America, threw bones at chance and became Crazy Horse killed by a lover.

9/64

Screw it all, I am not a pedigree. The grief of piecing together a race is crap, a few beads, a few feathers, a few million dead people. There isn't a need to go any further than the beauty of a bullet in the head.

I am 55/64 Lakota, 9/64 is my relief not to be an Indian, not to fear pow wows, or objectively look at Indian tacos. 9/64 doesn't worry about the rest of humanity, this is a calmness in selfishness.

The Indian wars still rage in me. I am termination's legacy. I let my diseases eat my mind. The imagination is the battlefield and I lie in its Midwest snowstorm. The one pose I often dance and end with is that last photograph of Chief Big Foot frozen with my dreams of dreaming I am safe and will live.

Lakotas Die in the Northwest

He had his hair in two long, wild braids down to his waist.

Always wore his best ribbon shirt. He shadow-boxed daily for an hour to keep his arms fit for 49er fights, or when he's at a drum with others. He would pound his drumstick with his stronger arm and would sing honor songs or sneak up songs. He kept a blue and white star quilt in his junked car trunk. He was ready for snagging.

At a pow wow in a gym, his head pulsed and the dance floor ached. He saw a dancer's foot lift off the ground, jump off this blue planet, dig into the earth meat. Living in the Northwest, he has learned to eat salmon.

Word came today that his biological father started his journey. He cut his hair in mourning and at the wake, he placed his braids in the casket. His braids were memories, he'd let them go and when his hair grew back, his grief would lessen. He would be someone he never knew.

He fell off a wagon he didn't know he was on. He drank to feel warm and numb, feel closer to the one he never loved: his father who he never wished to be. He uncomfortably passed out and slept without dreaming. Afraid-to-Love, Afraid-to-Live, Just-Afraid. He pondered surnames, pondered tombstones.

It was never over. The woman he loved left him. He thought of her naked body, pink lips and nipples, the taste of her neck, the taste of her saliva. He thought of her face with closed eyelids. Remembered the way their hair would tangle in each other.

Moonlight was too brilliant and rainy hours were too long. Nobody came with good songs or visited with funny stories. Water medicine didn't work well with sleeping pills or heroin. Orange juice and vodka hurt his kidneys and left his face numb. He turned his head to nobody in his bed or under his blankets. The white sheets he laid in were cold. Death was a realization he was alone in Portland.

Loves-to-Be-Afraid, Dreams-Without-Dreaming, Goes-Through-the-Motions-of-Existing, Sleeps-Without-Waking.

The Sleeping

My grandfather never mentioned anything about relocation or genocide, never about the "old ways," or stories involving tricksters. He spoke to me with glossed eyes blinking and spittle long off his chin.

"*Takoja*," he said. "I used to ride bare-back broncs."

He placed his right hand in front of his crotch in a fist, left hand opened in the air.

"*Takoja*, I'm a god-damn paratrooper." He fell to his knees, curled his body, and rolled.

He walked the streets of San Jose, CA, in worn cowboy boots with holes on the soles, trimmed cardboard slipped in the boots covering the openings. He wore a brown, felt, cowboy hat, blue jeans bought from K-Mart. He carried a brown paper bag wrapped around a bottle, black windbreaker found behind Goodwill, brown sleeping bag with well-storied stains in a new silver shopping cart.

"*Takoja*, you have French blood in you."

He would tease me. The wrinkle of his face would seem foreign when he smiled with most of his teeth missing and a faint rasped laugh. When he stayed with my family he mentioned how his dead wife would visit him and say it is time to go home. Some nights he moaned while my aunts would rub Icy-Hot into his muscles. It was a day without drink.

When he was on the wagon he would be quiet, cheerful, sometimes long in stare. He made sure to eat right and not have a low blood sugar count. He read the newspaper or watched the news on TV. He sat with one leg crossed over the other on the living room couch.

When I came home from school he would fold the newspaper, lay it on his lap, and have deep concern in his eyes.

"*Takoja wast'e*, how was your day?"

Some afternoons on the back porch with his one last lung, he would smoke Pall Malls sitting in a blue and white lawn chair. Mahtoway, the family dog, would lie at his side and let out small sighs when he talked to her in Lakota. With a slow brush of his hand down her back she'd place her head on his boots. He would sit outside until we turned on the porch light and he'd watch as much of the night come before it got too cold. Then he would stand, come back into the house, lay his bag on the guest room floor, and slip in to sleep.

Wounded Knee Opus

1.
Chief Big Foot

The horizon was on fire with blood, night sky, white snow, songs of a snowdrift like a blanket warping a melody. There was a crisp noise over a ridge and a vacant shine of a nearby creek.

He was propped up in an unwelcome pose, without the shards of ceremony. He was an image rustling and a rusted voice silenced. His skin was frozen and dark. His arm was reaching out and legs stepped to the side.

2.
Dance And They Will Vanish, Do This Else Disappear Yourself

Every Indian in the city wears a ghost shirt under urban ensembles.

This broken bottle world filled with spirits dancing around the blind, the liars and the thieves who talk with wind gusts and leaves turning. They all slowly scatter like imprints on concrete sidewalks.

Ghost shirt lives that walk between newspaper stand and trash can, between every layer of dust resting a short while on counter tops stained by coffee cups.

Ghost shirts are soft against the chest, ready to gather sweat when the dance begins.

Half-breeds try to cleanse the white out of their bodies while full bucks in their ghost shirts hold together their sanity.

If they danced it would be entertainment, an amusement on a street corner, not an act of survival or a lash of murder.

The street Indian is coldly dissected with anthropological eyes and handshakes that feel like warm blankets heavy with small pox. Eyes that spark like a dull report of a Hotchkiss gun, each shot and impact an angel who cawed for the first time or an owl that loudly in the cold sunrise flapped its wings little by little each day to the drums weighted with a haunted resonance.

Stationary Rescue

The feather bustles kaleidoscope at the college gym pow wow.

He walks up the bleachers and sees her. She waves him over and he walks toward her.

"Here," she says. "Come sit by me. You seem different. Stranger, empty, and not the good empty either."

He says, "I'm moving too fast to stand still."

"No, you are standing still, your eyes have rusted."

The swirling rainbow of feathers, the rustling bells, and children's laughter glow under florescent lighting. The singers and drums scratch out from a cheap P.A. system and dancers look out at the audience.

"It's okay if I stand for a while," he says. "It's okay to breathe differently the shadows that punch my face."

"Sit closer and tell me," she says.

He whispers in her ear, "I don't want life, but something is forcing me to stick around longer than I want."

"Well, in the meantime," she says, "sit next to me and then we'll get some coffee and talk a little longer."

"All right," he says, "but know I don't want anything a little longer."

The last hit of the drum rings out and children's round faces let out laughter in the silence. The dancers stand in a final dramatic pose.

Acts of Kindness

1.

"Is the store's hummus any good?"

The white lady behind me asked while we were in the checkout line. I was buying pita bread, hummus, and a half rack of beer.

"They are okay," I said. She laughed and repeated what I said.

She didn't know this was soft food that won't hurt much when I'm puking later that night. She didn't know that the check I was writing was made of rubber. She didn't know I was thinking of my grandfather's dialysis machine fears or my biological father's seizures and his diabetes.

Tonight I'll walk Alberta Street looking into store and gallery windows. I'll stop outside of Lillian Pitt's gallery and want to sleep in the doorway, to be as close and far away as I can from Indian people.

2.

I see my face's reflection in the window with the rest of the native art. I spit at my face and it quickly dries as it goes down the glass.

They would never know how a drunk, lonely night is ended and wished they never knew how it began.

I shiver as I take another sip of my refilled forty; my meal tonight is starting to turn. I have to go back to my apartment. I don't want to turn on the heat so I sit on the couch and sip beer. Nights alone are always okay when it's cold outside. My life is raw, cliché, and plastic. It's okay. I have until tomorrow to take care of what needs to be taken care of. I finish and throw my bottle across the room and sit in the dark.

December Seventh, Two Thousand and One

Friday, before midnight, I down two bottles of cheap red wine and
twenty sleeping pills. I sit on my living room couch and listen to
a record play the sounds of the ocean. I listen to the waves rolling,
seagulls scream, dogs barking, light rain, and the low hum of earth. I try
not to close my eyes else like waves crashing against rocks I'll spin out
of control.

My arms are heavy while I dial on the phone my second Ex.

"I did it," I say.

"No, Trevino," she says. "You said you wouldn't. You promised me."

"I tried..."

"Are you nodding off?" "...Yes."

"Stay awake Trevino." "Yes."

I hang up the phone, go to the bathroom, and throw up in the
toilet. I throw up bile, red wine, and half-dissolved pills. I sit on the
couch again. There's a knock on the front door, I don't move, the door
opens and two cops walk in. "How are you, Sir?" one cop says.

"Fine, very fine," I say.

I see paramedics attach electrode stickers to my chest. They put me
in an ambulance and try to make conversation with me. Next I'm in the
ER drinking charcoal water and trying to piss in a bottle. I hear
the heart pulse machine stop. A nurse checks the connections and it
beeps again.

They take me to a quiet room. The nurse says I'm low on potassium
and the I.V. might burn. It does, but as long as I can feel it, I don't care.
I look out the window and see Mt. Hood, long thin clouds, and the
horizon in pastels. The rising sun looks like an antique pocket watch
slowly pulled out of night.

"Why did you do it?" says the hospital psychiatrist. "Where's god?"
I say.

"Was it your girlfriend who called?"

I don't say anything and he leaves. I sleep a little until the I.V. starts to burn more and I wake. They say I can leave in a few hours. The nurse brings me breakfast, but I can't eat.

"Will you be all right?" the nurse asks.

"Yes," I say.

Early Saturday morning, I sign myself out of the hospital and sit at a bus stop. I'm not wearing any socks. My hands are shaky. I have a hangover. Everything I see is wobbly. I feel weak, but clear-headed and relieved. On the bus, children laugh, babies cry, and I nod off. I exit the bus and walk three blocks to my place. I am home. I turn on the living room stereo, sit on the couch, and fall asleep listening to the ocean.

About the Poet

Trevino L. Brings Plenty was born on the Cheyenne River Sioux Reservation, Eagle Butte, South Dakota, April 4, 1976. A Minneconjou Lakota Indian, he lived on the reservation until age three, then with family moved to the San Francisco Bay area. At age 16, he moved to Portland, Oregon, where he now resides. He is 55/64 Lakota, the 9/64 is unknown (probably fur trapper).

CPSIA information can be obtained at www.ICGtesting.com
Printed in the USA
LVOW042347190212

269408LV00001B/37/P